Love's Garden

Love's Garden
Naiya Smith

I dedicate this book to myself. No need to call it cocky, but self-love! I have come a long way!!!! Shout out to God.

-Sincerely, BLUE

I was standing in a crowd when I heard a woman ask, "whatever happened to Cupid?"

I laughed. Went to my rock and couldn't get her out my head. It takes a special person to show interest in your story. She reminded me of Love, which made me go back down memory lane. First thought was Love being cared for, then questioned, then punched, stabbed, cussed out, and finally, abandoned. Love is the cat who won't leave your porch.

She understands that she is needed in this world. She realizes that with her job, comes downfalls, but pays no mind to the bad because she knows that good is to come.

Did you know that Love needs you?

She needs you like Darius needed that poem to get Nina's attention, like Nisi and Mickey needed to know that even the hood has Black Princesses. Love needs you like Lucille needed Ray Bud to act right when Junior and Charisse had to come stay with them, like Big Worm needed Smokey to give him his money, like Mookie needed to get off crack, like Black folks need to know all the black classics.

Loves place in the world is secure. She is the glue black girls wish for when they have a quick weave, the du-rag black boys beg for when they want waves, the toys kids ask for when Christmas is near, the new pair of Jordan's folks stand in line for on Saturdays, the education parents pay for when College comes. Love is the knee that holds you when you pray, the candle that guides you when the storm turns off the lights, the Coco Butter that cures you when your brown becomes white; she is the Robitussin you need when you can't breathe out ya nose, the condom when health is cared for, the wisdom when Life kicks yo ass.

But a coward won't know a thing about Love. Mo and Q; case 16:20? I'd never claim them to be cowards; just young. But Love is about growth; learning yourself. Being honest with your heart and honestly, I appreciate the truth. Takes a strong woman to be patient with someone like me…someone like us. Love's "dopeness" is on a whole 'notha level.

Peep the story. Started with Mo and Q.

They met in their Universities Library. Q was walking through the second floor, when he noticed Mo sitting at one of the tables. She was working on a paper for one of her English classes. He wondered if he should approach her. God pushed his back, causing his feet to move.

"Hey." he stood in front of her.

She put her head up, "Hey."

"Q." he extended his hand.

"Mo." she shook it.

When their hands parted, Q stood there silently. Mo looked at him, wondering 'what the hell does he want'.

"*So?*" she asked.

"Oh, I've…seen you at a couple parties. You hang with Lex, right?"

"Yeah, that's my girl."

"Word", he nodded his head, "Me and Lex from the same home town."

"Oh, that's what's up."

Butterflies don't affect Q like others; he uses them as encouragement.

Getting Mo's number was the challenge. She isn't one to share her personal space because, as she says, "People get on her damn nerves", but Q likes challenges.

Having mutual friends helped their interactions continue. If Q wasn't staring at Mo, he was picking at her.

"Why you babysittin' that drink?" he asked at a Social Event.

"Why you all up in my mix?" she rolled her neck.

He smiled; "I like you Mo."

"I can tell. You're always bothering me."

"Just try'na make you laugh."

"...but...you're not funny."

"I can make you laugh!" he said.

"No."

"How about you give me your number, so I can text you a joke."

"Or, or...or, you could leave me alone."

"What's wrong with a little conversation?"

"You get on my nerves Q!"

"But I'm cool people", he said, "Look, if you give me your number, I promise not to blow you up. I just want get to know you."

Though Q was annoying, Mo found him charming, so she gave him her number. Plus, she knew how to block calls and text, so if the situation called for it, she knew what to do!

...and just like Q said, he sent her a joke.
'Knock, knock', he text.
'Nah...aint nobody home', she responded.
'Act accordingly Mo.'
She laughed, but he didn't know it.

The text messages became frequent.
Entertaining. Q was really into her.

He'd text her in the Morning to make sure
her day started off right.

Ask her 'how her classes were', and Mo
don't really rock with school, so she had a lot to
say.

'Me and one of my Professors got into it',
she messagcd Q.

'Why?' he asked.

"Cause he kept calling my name and I did
not feel like being bothered'.

Took no time for Mo to be the one making Q
laugh. She was blunt; meant no harm, but refused
to apologize if feelings were hurt.

'Why you cuss people out so much?' he
asked.

'Folks swear sticks and stones break their
bones, so I figured a cuss out is better than an ass
whoopin'.' She answered.

'Yo, you got issues.'

'Makes sense to me.'

Q peeped that Mo took no shit, so he figured if she was entertaining him, she found him interesting.

'How big you crushin' on me?' he questioned.

'Who said I was crushin'?'

'...tell me you don't feel nothin'.'

'You're cool, but I don't know you like that.'

'Mo, as much as we're around each other, you don't know me like that?'

'Not one on one.'

'Then let's do something one on one.'

'Aight.'

Pockets were looking funny, so they had a night in. Q let her pick the Movie while he asked questions.

"How many siblings do you have?"

"Seven." she answered.

"Dayumm."

She laughed; "Chill, most come from my Daddy."

He appreciated her facial expression, "Ask me some questions."

"Who's your favorite artist?" Mo sat up.

"Cole."

She nodded her head.

Her heart belonged to Chance the Rapper but every now and then, she allowed J. Cole to enter her personal space.

"What's your favorite Movie?" she continued.

"Menace II Society."

She gasp. College taught Mo that all black folks weren't raised to appreciate the Black Classics. "Yes." She said under her breath.

"What?" Q smiled.

"Finally."

Sex and Mo had been strangers for months. She spent that time learning her body, and though she was accomplishing a lot, a man's touch was needed. Q was chosen by default.

She hit him up, saying 'she wanted to *chill*'.

He told her 'he'd be there in thirty minutes'.

While taking a shower, red invaded her wash cloth. Aunt Flo gave no heads up about an early arrival.

"Really?" Mo smacked her teeth.

She was hot! She couldn't call Q and cancel, so she finished washing and got dressed.

Childish is what she classified herself as. It was one in the Morning, she was going to a guy's house, but was unable to have sex!

"I'm outside." Q text her.

Disappointed, she left her Dorm and went to his car.

That was the first night Mo entered his Bedroom. It had the usual stuff; full size bed, two dressers, and a night stand.

She noticed that he had clothes piled up in the corner.

"You don't have a dirty clothes hamper?" she asked.

"Those are clean clothes." he answered.

"Wow."

He let her pick what she wanted to watch while ho rollod thc blunt.

"I see why everybody watch Martin." She said while flipping through the channels.

"Why?" he asked.

"Cause it's the only black show on TV!"

"It's a funny show."

"It is."

They didn't talk much, just chilled. Let the TV be the entertainment of the room while they got comfortable in the clouds.

Mo wondered how shit was gone play when they got in bed.

"Lord, please don't let Q try something cause I'll hate to have to explain what is going on." She prayed in her head.

Though God heard her prayers, that wasn't why Q didn't try anything. He put his hormones aside to show how much he liked her.

Chivalry is not dead.

Claimin' jones was something Mo wasn't with; admiration was what she called it. She liked that he enjoyed her presence. She digged that even in a crowd, their eyes would connect. Her spot was becoming permanent in his bed. He'd keep her ear rings together so that when she came back, they would be paired. He looked out for her. Anytime one of her bobby pins stuck out of her hairstyles, he'd push it back in. He learned that at night she'd put her glasses on the floor, so he started getting up and putting them on his night stand. He let her sleep with the thick pillow. He noticed that she'd sweat during the night, so he'd let the fan focus on her. His arms protected her from the dark.

And even though Q was causing Mo to feel like she mattered, she walked with Fear. I didn't agree, but understood. Working with humans meant I watched ya'll; quickly learned that a clock is given credit for Love. But the truth is, Love knows no time. All she knows is how much a person can give, and if she notices that someone is half ass'n, she puts in work.

But let me continue with Mo and Q's honey moon stage.

"You scared I'ma hurt you?" Q asked.

"Nah", she answered, "Scared I'ma hurt you."

Don't let the Devil know ya Fears. He'll use 'em against you.

They spent a lot of time together.

I remember their first kiss. Q wanted Mo to scoot over on the bed, but she wouldn't, so he threatened to kiss her lips. She didn't move, so he made it a promise.

She stayed there.

So, he did it again.

Corny.

But he got to kiss her.

Aunt Flo had been gone for a minute, so Mo was back to her mission. Q's hands started touching her, but not where she wanted. He liked to rub her back.

One night, Mo told him 'You're rubbin' the wrong spot'.

That was the statement Q was waitin' for. Took his hands no time to do what she dreamed of.

Not only was Q a respectful man, but he was a man who loved the body of a woman. He studied them with his eyes. Only black women got his Love cause that's what he was connected to. Saw 'em as Queens, cause, in his words, "A black woman got hella sauce; extra sauce; that saucy sauce."

He let his hands explore every part of her body. Nothing was off limits.

He licked his lips while looking at Mo's eternity. Before showing her how much of a man he was, told her "not to run".

"I don't run."

"Oh", he chuckled, "A'ight."

She tried to run.

Now, usually both folks are hit at the same time, but Mo and Q were different. Q was open to his feelings; therefore, he was the first to get hit.

One night he asked Mo, "Why you always got 'cha back to me?"

She looked over her shoulder; "I don't know."

He opened his arms; "Come 'mere."

She did so.

Watching Mo rest her head on Q's chest gave me the chills.

He kissed her on the forehead; "I got you, aight?"

"A'ight."

Maybe Mo thought he was playin', but I saw him Sparkle. Target #1 was hit.

Believe it or not, Q made it easy for Mo to sparkle. It wasn't that he had to prove himself, but he had to show her something to believe in. All her life she had been around relationships that either failed, or looked successful with hella lies behind them. Long ago, Mo decided that she'd rather fantasize about Love than experience it. Like the manuscript said, 'You wanna make God laugh, tell Him your plans'.

You see, Q was showing Mo new things. He had her feeling all...giggly inside. This was the first guy who kept her interest; the first guy to let her know he was feelin' her. A Kehlani "The Way" type of man.

Mentally. Physically. Emotionally. Q touched Mo in ways his hands couldn't; it was the simple things that made her question the purpose of her walls.

Mo was hit the night she talked to God about Q. Sinful, it may be, but after sex she prayed, "Lord, please let me know if this man is for me".

Mo sparkled brighter than Q had.

I think it was because Q showed her who he was. A simple man, who was attractive, down with enjoyin' the 'erb, could chill and say absolutely nothing, got her whatever she wanted, loved kissing her forehead, smiled while talking about his

Grandma, was down with education, the first one to lend a hand, knew how to touch her, good at listening, and made sure she was okay.

She digged him as a person. That's where Love starts.

They were good, until the night Q's phone rung at two in the morning. Didn't answer until the person called the third time. Mo could hear the females voice.

She knew of his friend girls, and though she didn't agree with it, she never spoke up. For the most part, none of them crossed any boundaries, until that night! She wanted to say something, let him know that when a certain hour hits, female friends should know not to call, but because her feelings weren't equivalent to her position, she remained quiet.

Q got off the phone and tried to pull Mo close to him. She wasn't with the shits.

"Yo, you're really not fuckin' with me?" he asked.

She ignored him.

There was no kissin' or lovin' that night. He stayed on one side of the bed and she stayed on the other.

The next day, Mo went back to her Dorm and vented to her roommate, Ciara.

"But it was a friend that called. Did the conversation sound too friendly?" Ciara asked.

"No, but what bothers me is…. that her calling bothered me. I'm not even with this dude and my feelings for him are real." Mo responded.

"What's wrong with feeling, sum'n?"

"Getting hurt."

"So, you're gonna end it before ya'll can start? Why don't you just talk to him about it? He can't read ya mind."

Mo didn't want to have that conversation with Q because she didn't want him to know how much she cared.

Summer came. It was time for Mo to leave her Dorm and head back her city.

Going home meant Q wouldn't be around. Mo thought it would give her the opportunity to dead her feelings. Silly child. Absence makes the heart grow fonder.

Late nights started getting to her. Q's arms were no longer in reach. Soon Mo remembered that she was afraid of the dark. Not because of monsters, but because of death. Being alone in a room when it was dark outside, made her think of a casket. Q had learned that secret a long time ago.

"Stop focusing on death baby. Your position in my future is secure." she reminisced on his words.

Their communication was slowing down. Mo finally found a dude who had no problem calling her first, but she forgot that guys like to be called too.

The only time she'd call was when she wanted to discuss some real shit.

The first phone call of the summer started the downfall. You see, even though Mo was trying to kill her feelings for Q, she felt loyalty to him. So much that when her old boo, Jay, tried to hang out with her, she'd turn him down.

"You're being loyal to someone you don't even talk to on a daily." One of her sisters called out.

"I feel how I feel." she responded.

"How does he feel?" her sister asked.

"I don't know."

"Ask him."

Mo decided to call Q. Instead of asking him, like her sister said, she came up with a hypothetical question.

"Hypothetically, if two people are talking and one begins talking to someone else, does the other person have the right to be upset?" she asked.

"Not if they don't have any boundaries." he replied.

She got quiet.

"Why you ask?" he questioned.
"Just a scenario."

Mo took his answer and ran with it. Figured that he didn't care about her.

What got on my nerves was her delivery. She should've been straight up with the purpose of her question. To Q, the question wasn't about them, so neither was his answer.

...anyhow...Mo hit Jay up. Let him know that she wanted to hang out. With no hesitation, he came to get her. She thought Jay would be able to get Q out her head.

Hella wrong!

Whole time, she was comparin' the two. Jay wasn't holding the steering wheel like Q would, his seat wasn't back far enough, his music choice was trash, and he did not rap along to the right songs. Everything got on her nerves!

When they got to Jays place, Mo headed to the Livingroom.

"You don't want to go to my room?" he asked.

"Nah." She answered.

He followed behind. They sat beside one another on the couch. Jay's hands acted as magnets to her legs.

"Let's keep our hands to ourselves." She moved them.

"Mo, I missed you. I can't keep my hands to myself." he told her.

"Then you're gonna have to take me home because I just wanna watch TV."

"Okay, okay. I'll keep 'em to myself." he gave in.

For a minute, he was good. Occasionally, he'd look at her.

"You a'ight Mo?" he noticed her sparkle.

"Yeah." She refused to look at him.

"Mo", he touched her face and tried to kiss her. She moved her head, rejecting his lips. He knew the sparkle wasn't for him.

"Yo, who is he?" Jay knew it was someone else.

"I don't think you want to talk about it." She responded.

"It aint none of my homies, is it?" he asked.

"Nah", she shook her head, "But it is someone."

"Who?"

"You don't know him." She took a deep breath.

"Whoever this nigga is, is making it impossible for me to touch you Mo."

She could tell his feelings were hurt.

"Let's be truthful Jay, we stopped talking a while ago." Mo reminded him.

"Yeah, but when did that allow you to meet a new dude?"

"Allow?", Mo paused and looked at him, "You know what happened? You worked to get me, and when you got me you forgot."

"Forgot what?"

"Who the hell I was! Remember when I asked you to let me know I mean something to you?"

Jay sat there silently.

Mo laughed, "You flipped the hell out. Told me you 'weren't gonna chase me'."

"So, what you sayin'? One man's trash is another man's treasure."

"If we were talkin' about trash we could use that quote, but since we're talking about me; one man's lost is another one's gain."

Mo made me proud. I mean, she broke Jay's heart, but she stood up for herself. It's magical when a woman knows her worth.

Jay left Mo's mind when he got out of her sight.

Who took over it? Q. His answer. Her feelings.

Stupid was an understatement to what Mo called herself. "I broke all of my rules for him! I put down walls for him." She confessed to her same sister.

"Well how many walls you got, because it seems to me that some are still up." Her sister responded.

"Shut up Key'."

While Mo was trippin', Q was wondering why he hadn't heard from her.

"Why 'ont you just call her?" Q's homeboy, Ryan, suggested while they played "the game".

"Cause Man…I'm not about to be the one whose always callin'. She got me lookin' thirsty."

His homeboy laughed; "You aint care about lookin' thirsty before."

"Yeah but…before, I was just crushin'. I'm kinda feelin' her now."

"Aint no *kinda*. Call your girl." Ryan won the game, "And since I beat you, you gotta do it."

That night, he made the phone call.

"You miss me?" Q asked Mo.

"Yeah." she responded.

"Then why don't you call?"

"...cause I don't know if you'll be busy." she answered.

"Mo, come on now...if I'm not at work and you call me, you know I'll answer."

She stayed quiet.

"But I miss you", he continued, "How it feels to sleep alone?"

"...lonely."

"I feel you."

They fell asleep on the phone.

A part of me wished that Q sparkled for someone ...who made it easier for him.

"Mo's giving him a hard time." I vented to God.

He laughed; "She's giving him *a time*."

Mo tried...I'll give her that, but she still walked with Fear.

"Come see me for the weekend." Q suggested.

With no hesitation, she bought a train ticket. While on it, she wondered if she'd wasted her money, remembering that Q "didn't care if she talked to other people".

"Mo, just have a good time." She remembered her sister's encouragement.

"It's just Q. Just…relax." She repeated to herself.

Her nerves went ghost till the train stopped at her destination. She had gas.

The train station wasn't packed, so it took no time for Mo to reach Q.

A little secret? Q was just as nervous as she was. Butterflies let him know that they never left.

When Mo reached him, they were both cheesin'.

She slid in between his arms and gave him a hug.

"I missed you." He kissed her forehead.

"I missed you too." She kissed his lips.

They held onto one another long enough for folks to start looking. Q loves the smell of shea butter and berries, so her hair being in his nose didn't bother him.

Natural hair is dope.

"How was the ride?" he touched her puff.

"It was cool."

They let go of one another.

He grabbed her bags; "Give me another kiss."

She did so.

"You hungry?" he asked.

She laughed; "Yeah. Can you make me some noddle's?"

He smiled; "I bought some just for you."

He put his arm around the back of her neck and pulled her close. "I'm glad you're here."

"Me too."

Riding in his car reminded her of what home felt like.

"I missed you." She repeated.

He smiled; "You sayin' it like you're for real."

"I am!"

They got to a red light. Mo touched Q's left cheek, moved his head to hers, and kissed him. It wasn't a little kiss either; more like "I'ma tare dat ass up" type of kiss.

"You missed me, huh?" he smiled when their lips parted.

"Hell yeah."

They got to his Apartment. Q got her bags out the car.

"Such a man." She smiled at him.

They headed up the stairs. She idolized his body while he walked in front of her. She was feenin'.

He unlocked the door and allowed her to walk in first.

"It smells like Sunflower seeds in here." Mo said.

"You always say that." Q stood behind her.

They went to his bedroom. His clothes were in their usual spot.

"Why don't you fold your clothes?" Mo asked.

"Takes too long", he put her luggage on the floor, "Why'd you bring so many bags?"

"Didn't know what I'd need."

"Uhm", he kissed her lips, "Wanna smoke?"

"Hell yeah."

They both laughed.

He reached in his pocket and pulled out a blunt.

"I knew I smelled weed. You brought that in the train station?! You crazy as hell."

"Aint nobody say nothing." He went to his night stand and picked up a white lighter.

"You know white lighters are bad luck?" she asked.

"I'm not superstitious." He lit the blunt and took a couple hits.

"Okay, when shit starts going wrong, know its cause of that lighter."

"Yeah, whatever." He sat on his bed.

He handed Mo the blunt. Mo stood in front of him as she smoked. Q put his hands on her waist. All he could do was smile.

"What?" she asked.

"I missed yo' mean ass."

"Me? Mean?" she touched her chest.

"Yes, you!" he opened his low eyes.

She smiled, "I missed your annoyin' ass."

He started laughing.

Mo tried to step back from Q, but he had a strong grip on her waist.

"Let me sit down!" she demanded.

"Nah", he shook his head while looking at her pants button, "Stand in front of me."

Her panties got wet.

He took the blunt from her.

"I wasn't done." she said.

Q ignored her. He put the blunt out in his ashtray. Mo took that as an opportunity to step back.

Q stood up and placed his hands back on her; "Give me another kiss."

She did so. He let it be known that her lips weren't leaving his. His hands went from her breast, to stomach, to waist, to ass, to her pants button.

"Hold on Q." Mo remembered she was supposed to be mad.

He ignored her and started kissing her neck.

That being Mo's spot messed her up.

Q picked her up and placed her on the bed. Mo looked at him as she laid on her back. While kissing on her neck, he began unbuttoning her pants.

"Q." she touched his chest. He ignored her. She repeated herself.

"What's up?"

"If I talk to someone, you won't be mad?" she asked.

He looked at her; "You aint talkin' to nobody but me."

"Then why did you answer my hypothetical question like that?"

He kissed her lips; "It's only me and you Mo."

"So, what we doing?"

"Talking."

She looked at him; "Just us?"

"Just us."

"Don't say that just cause you're in between my legs!"

He kissed her lips; "I promise."

She smiled at her.

"Now, you gonna let me take ya pants off?" he asked.

"Yeah." She nodded her head.

Q showed Mo how much he missed her.

They rested beside each other like they were the only things that mattered. Q couldn't help but spoon Mo's body while his arm rested on her side. Nothing else but the street lights seeped into the room.

"What you thinkin' about?" Q asked.

"Nothin'." She answered.

He kissed her cheek.

She slid back closer to him while inhaling his scent.

As peaceful as they looked, I saw Fear walking around the room. Usually, Fear stands beside the person who allows him in, but if everyone in the room accepts him, he moves freely.

"What you doin' here?" I asked him.

"I was invited!" he answered.

"An invitation doesn't mean you have to come."

"Well I'm here; and aint leavin' till they tell me to do so."

Beating Fears ass wouldn't make him leave, so I told Mo and Q to 'talk about what's botherin' them'.

The only person to budge was Mo.

"What you want from this Q?" she asked.

"What you mean?" he tightened his arm around her.

"I'm cool with *talking,* but...I'm asking about longevity. Are we working towards anything?"

"I have an internship in a couple months. I don't want to start something, not knowing how it will end." His arm loosened. That helped her push it off and turn around, so they could talk face to face.

"So, we are what we will be?"

"I don't want you to say it like that, but...my mind isn't with a relationship."

"But we said that we're only talking to each other. That's a form of commitment."

"Mo, I'm not saying I want to mess with other people."

"But you don't want...to be in a relationship?"

"We're about to let this conversation ruin our night?" he sat up.

"I'm not letting it ruin the night, but I'm asking a question. If we're not going anywhere, I can't invest my time in this." She followed his movement.

They looked at each other.

"Mo, I can't tell you what to do." He told her.

She looked to the left and then back at Q; "Then I can't do this." She got out his bed and began putting on her clothes.

He stood up and came over to her; "Mo, where you going?"

"I'ma call my cousin. She stays up the street." She refused to let tears fill her eyes.

He grabbed her pants, "Damn baby, I know you want us to end, but can we at least have this last night?"

"No Q", she looked at him, "We can't. How you gonna get my hopes up and then say, 'you don't want a relationship'?"

"You're making it seem like I don't care."

"Do you?!"

"Duh Mo!"

"Q don't 'duh' me. Keep it real with you, I feel like you're hittin' me with a whole bunch of bullshit", she yanked her pants from him, "*So* you can kiss my ass!"

"Yo, you're mad because I don't want us to end badly?"

"You are focusing on an ending to something that hasn't even started. I'll be damned to vibe with someone who doesn't think I'm worth a risk. You got me fucked up."

"Your attitude is unnecessary as hell. I think you need to chill."

The biggest mistake a man can ever do is tell a woman to chill when she's mad.

"Q, I want you to step back from me." She gave him a look that let him know she wasn't playing.

"Mo, you got me fucked up if you think you 'bout to leave like this."

"Like what? Like this aint worth my time, cause clearly it aint."

"Yo", he stepped back from her, "If you want to leave you can."

"Say less!"

Q went to his bathroom while Mo grabbed all her stuff. She called her cousin, letting her know she needed a ride. Cuzo was there less than five minutes.

Lauryn Hill once said: You let go and I'll let go too.

My purpose of speaking wasn't for them to end, but to talk. Humans idolize Fear because they live with Excuses. Q didn't want to get into a relationship because he "didn't know how they'd end" while Mo wanted a relationship to give purpose to her feelings. Fear moved with both of 'em.

I asked God 'what was the purpose'. He told me to 'Trust Him'.

We parted.

I went back to my Rock and stared at my bow and arrows, wondering if it was time to give it up.

"Gideon did it too, you know?" Love's voice came from behind.

I turned around and saw her approaching.

"Did what?" I asked, getting up so she could sit down.

"Had doubt in God." She copped a squat.

"I don't have doubt in God. I have doubt in His choices."

"So, you can judge?" she asked.

"I believe in those kids, Love." I said, referring to Mo and Q.

"So, do I."

"They are failing. Mo walked away, and Q let her."

Love looked at her hands. In the left was Mo and right, Q. "Looks like they made a mistake."

"Hell yeah, they made a mistake!" I threw my bow and arrow.

"But look", she stood up and came over to me. She showed me her hands, "They're still sparklin'."

I looked and saw what she spoke of; "What is the value of a sparkle if they don't believe in it?"

"To teach them."

"Love, I'm here to tell you if all of this is for a lesson---"

"Then what? You just gonna quit?" she interrupted me, "I dare you."

Love may be a small woman, but she intimidated me.

"My girl Jill said, 'The sky aint a ceiling'. Tell me you didn't stop believin'." Love hoped.

"I stopped having a reason to."

Love looked at me and shook her head, "I gotta go."

I'm sure she was disappointed, but at the time, I didn't care. I was tired of believing in a lost cause.

While writing my two weeks' notice, Job entered my personal space.

"My mans, announce yourself before you sneak up on someone." I told him.

"What's your issue with God?" He asked.

"He made Hope look different. He knew they were gonna do that and said nothing while I idolized them."

"I remember that frustration."

I looked at Job, remembering his story; "Nah man, my problem has nothing on what you went through. I don't even know how you made it."

"The Lord giveth and the Lord taketh away."

"You say it so easily." I noticed.

"Because I know my friend." He sat down beside me, "Cupe, if all you're doing is looking at what's in front of you, you'll falsely convict God."

"But I don't understand Job. Mo and Q aren't the only ones that have been failing, and God is a God who knows, so why is He allowing me to have Faith in this? He is the main one always talking about believing in something, yet knows that there is nothing to believe in. God use to be my friend."

"You lack knowledge Cupe."

"God aint sayin' nothin'."

"He doesn't have to!"

I gave no response.

I didn't turn in my resignation Letter. I also didn't go and talk to God. I just stuck to my job. Didn't allow my feelings to get involved with my clients. If I saw a sparkle, I hit them and kept going about my business.

Mo and Q didn't enter my mind until I received a letter in the mail. There wasn't an envelope or stamp; just a piece of Notebook paper folded with jagged edges still on it.

To: Cupid
From: Mo

My heart dropped. I didn't know if it were smart to read or ignore it. My fingers didn't care what I choose, took 'em less than a second to unfold the letter.

Yo Cupid,

I don't know if you exist or if any of this is of your doing, but if so...do me a favor and stay away. I don't mean for this letter to be rude, but honest. This nigga didn't even care to try! And I know you watched it.

So, stay the hell away from me.

-Mo.

With no hesitation, I went to God.

Before any words could be said, I handed Him the letter.

"She's questioning my existence and is mad at me about something *she* did!" I yelled.

"Yeah…that's how they do." God nodded His head.

"What is the point?! I am shooting arrows, and no one is entertaining them!"

"Ignoring a blessin', huh?"

"Yeah! I'm not doing this no more." I handed God my bow and arrows, "I'm out."

"Lettin' it go?" God asked.

"Yes…I am."

God nodded His head, "So shall it be."

I turned away from Him.

"But", He stopped me, "you have a year to come back and get them. After a year, they're going to someone else."

"God, I don't care." I continued walking.

Love ran up to me, "What you call yourself doing?!"

"Leaving." I paid her no mind.

"You're giving up on me? What makes you better than Mo and Q?" she grabbed my arm to stop me.

I looked at her, "I'm not giving up on you; I'm giving up on them experiencing you. I'm tired of my hopes going in vain."

"Do something for me Cupid." She said.

"What?"

"Watch Mo and Q for a year."

I chuckled, "God has given me a year of vacation and you think I want to spend that time watching Mo and Q?"

"Yes. If after a year you don't want your bow and arrow, I'll.... go on a date with you."

I rose my eyebrows; "Promise."

"I never lie."

So, I was back to watching Mo and Q. Though things were over with them, Q would still text her to see how she was doing. Mo was working on her character, so she'd text him back.

The closer school came, the more Mo thought about how it'd be when her and Q see each other. She had been learning that Love doesn't leave when you end a situation, nor does she care that you haven't claimed her. Love likes to whisper, and you ignoring her does not hurt her feelings. Love's patience helps her remember that all of this is bigger than her; that God had a plan in mind when He paired you with someone who has the ability to scratch below the surface.

Love scratches act differently to the skin. Acts as an infection if you ignore it. It'll itch. Pus. Grow. And Neosporin can't help. It's this thing called the Truth that you'll need to cure it. Best thing about it is, you don't need a prescription; just a conversation with your heart.

But Mo wasn't ready to be honest with herself. Being honest about feelings meant being vulnerable and reality is, people don't find Love valuable enough to expose themselves.

Love is magical. The pizazz this world needs to add light. A person sparkling is never overlooked because light hits them in a way that exposes their Jones to the world. Why you think

Savon could tell that Darius was stuck on Nina? Why you think Nina's home girl Josie could tell that her and Darius fucked the night before? Or to make Darius mad, Hollywood took Nina on a date? It's funny how everyone else can notice the Love Jones except the folks experiencing it.

Crazy how Love can change your vision. See, at first you become blind, but the more you sacrifice things, the more you can see. And I'm not talking about sacrificing your peace of mind or self-respect, because I don't pair you with nothing but Love, I'm talking about sacrificing every thought of what could go wrong. About allowing Love to show you wings you didn't know were there.

"How are you going to get these kids to admit to you?" I asked Love as Mo's family packed up the Moving truck.

"With God's help." She answered.

Mo was back in town, but she didn't tell Q. Had to get her mind right before seeing him.

She had made the decision to end them, because she felt like he was making her choose between him and herself. Long ago, her Mama made her and some of her sisters analyze Tamia's song 'Me', so picking herself was taught. But the repercussions of her action were hitting her hard.

While fixing up her room, she thought of how much more fun it'd be if Q was there. Give her someone to talk shit to; to kiss on when the music changed from The Notorious B.I.G to Musiq Soulchild. But, she had to act unbothered, so she allowed loneliness to continue.

"I'm having something at my spot tonight", Lex called her, "Come through."

"A'ight." Mo responded.

Ciara hadn't gotten to their Apartment yet. Mo figured by the time she came back; her girl would be there, and the AC would be comfortable at her crib.

Lex didn't invite a lot of folks, only the people she rocked with extra hard. Meaning, Q was there.

Mo sat on the couch with some other people, while Q stood in the kitchen. She could see him looking at her from the corner of her eye, but made it seem like her focus was with the conversations close to her.

"Talk to them Love." I said.

"They aint ready to listen." She responded.

Q was keepin' his distance. He could tell Mo still had a little attitude, but once liquor hit his system, he saw through that.

"Why you been ignoring me?" he asked her.

"What you talkin' 'bout?" Mo acted clueless.

"You haven't said shit to me all night."

She shrugged her shoulders.

"You don't have to be mean all the time Mo."

"I'm not being mean. I'm giving you what you asked for."

"What I ask for?"

"Independence." She rolled her neck.

He laughed; "Yo, you're *still* trippin'."

"I think not." She walked away from him.

The South put flava in Mo. I'm not one to encourage attitudes, but hers was a little entertaining. Made Mo and Q more interesting to watch.

Q didn't leave her alone. Mo didn't want to show out, so she headed home.

Seeing Ciara's car in the parking lot had her hype. She rushed into their spot. Ciara was in the kitchen, sitting on the counter.

"My bitch!" she smiled at Cee.

"What it do!" Cee lifted her arms.

"Oh, how I missed you!" she closed the door behind her.

"Where yo ass been? I got here bout two hours ago!"

Mo explained the get together. Told about how Q kept bothering her.

"What the hell happened with ya'll?" Cee asked.

Mo told the story.

"What? Ya'll ended cause of what?"

Mo repeated herself.

Cee shook her head; "All ya'll need is a little communication."

"Fuck that."

She hopped off the counter top; "You try'na smoke? Got some shit from this plug up North."

"I'm with it."

When the Morning came, Mo was on Q's mind. He hit her up to see if they could talk. Not only did she ignore the call, but when he text her, she didn't hit him back.

"I think Mo fuckin' with somebody else." He told Ryan.

"Ask her."

But he didn't. Q wasn't about to ask a question Mo actions seemed to answer, so he assumed that he was right. He also wasn't with sitting around thinking about someone who had moved on, so he found a distraction. A new girl.

Lex relayed the information to Mo.

"Keep it real with you Lex, I got other things to tend to." Mo responded.

And she was telling the truth. Life was pokin' at Mo. Her school was holding her refund check, so her pockets were light as hell.

"I have rent, I have a car note, my phone is messing up, I have books I need to pay for, access codes I have to get; I promise I have no time to give Q attention."

Love rubbed Mo's back while she cried. Writing down things you need to pay for is discomforting when you have no money for it.

"Lord, there is no way you brought me this far for this to be as far as I can go." She prayed.

God remained silent while holding onto her hand.

One of her Professors gave her encouragement without even knowing; "Life is hard, and there will come times when giving up is easier than working for what you want, but I want ya'll to remember that you are the decedents of the slaves they couldn't kill. Don't let no one tell you what you can't do."

So, Mo went home and had a conversation with her storm. Told it that 'God build a fence around her, and no wind can move it'.

She gave me chills.

Hard times teach you about yourself, about your Faith, and dedication. You see, Mo was keeping Faith in God while I was wondering 'why was she talking to someone who wasn't speaking back'.

"Who said He isn't talking?" Love asked me.

"You heard Him say something?"

"You don't know how God works."

But I was learning. Mo was the teacher.

It got to a point where she wasn't opening Mail. She was ignoring what she didn't have, and said 'when she gets it, she'll handle it."

Even Ciara couldn't see her storm. She kept her emotions to herself; handed them to God before she went to sleep.

Her school gave her a percentage of her check. She took a deep breath, trying to stay calm. She got in her car and drove to the Treasurer's office. Before going in, she had to talk to herself; "Now Mo, remember we are trying to work on our character. We can't go in here and tare stuff up, cause that's not how adults act. Adults stay calm, so stay calm."

"Lord, I hope she acts right." Love said.

"I hope *they* act right." I added.

Mo got out of her car and went into the building. Love and I followed behind.

Mo's University has the tendency of giving her the run around, so I knew she was gonna exchange some words when she went inside.

"Listen to me ma'am, this money isn't for a shopping spree. I have things I need to pay for. How can I be successful when I don't have the money to buy the things I need?" she said to one of the workers.

"We gave you a percentage."

Mo looked at the woman for a while; "How would ya'll act if I gave ya'll a percentage? What is a percentage? If students at this University don't pay their complete bill when it is due, classes are dropped, housing is taken away, and cars are towed. Ma'am, I need my money in my bank account by Friday. No later. I have been very, very patient with ya'll, but the games are over. I'm serious Ma'am."

The woman noticed how serious Mo was, so she helped her out. Wrote a number down on a sticky note and told her to make the phone call.

"Thank you." Mo stood up.

"Good luck this school year."

"Why didn't God supply Mo with an Umbrella?" I asked Love.

"Cause Faith is her protection." She answered.

God eased up on her after a while. Mo was getting back to relaxing, meditating, enjoying the 'erb. Home girl was the hood version of a hippie; instead of listening to nature songs when she meditated, she was bumpin' Tupac.

Even had Ciara jump on board. Added her weed to the mix.

"Yo, how long you meditate?" Ciara asked.

"Till I fall asleep!"

Changed up their spot. Added incents, dream catchers, candles, and pillows.

Mo invited her girls over to experience her new lifestyle.

Five pillows were spaced out in the Livingroom. Blunts were rolled and placed in the middle of the floor. Her speakers were ready.

"Nice to see you're in a better mood." Mia, one of her other friends, said while walking into the Apartment.

"Thank you, thank you."

Lex looked around; "Mo, when did you become all Earthy?"

"My third eye."

Ciara walked into the room, dressed like Erykah Badu. Head wrap and dress.

"Ya'll asses rest in the clouds." Lex walked to one of the pillows. She sat down. "How you do this?!"

The session was going well. Fear left the room. Pain was dismissed. And Worry wasn't even allowed in.

"Folks need people like Mo." Love said.

I noticed Lex opening her right eye and looking at Mo.

"What she got to say?" I asked Love.

"Lex? Oh, she got the tea."

Lex slid over to Mo; "Yo, step outside with me real quick."

"What?" Mo looked at her.

"Come on." Lex stood up and grabbed Mo's hand. Quietly, they got up and went outside.

"What's up?" Mo asked her.

"On the real Mo, how you been?"

"Good."

"You talked to Q?"

"Nah, aint really had time to."

"...you know he got a girl, right?"

Her eyebrows rose; "He got a what?"

"I aint try'na mess up ya mood, but I know how ya'll were."

Mo rolled her eyes; "Man, I don't care."

Lex knew Mo was lying, but allowed her to stick with it; "A'ight; just making sure you're good."

"I appreciate you girl."

Mo allowed her mind to relax for the rest of the night, but the next morning…the original Mo was back!

She called Q. When he saw her name on his phone, his heart stopped.

He answered.

"I am sure that your pants are on fire with ya lyin' ass! You told me you didn't want to be in a relationship, whole while, you just didn't want to be with me. Got you a lil' girlfriend, huh?!"

"First of all, I'm not a liar and second, who told you?"

"Fuck your first of all, second of all, all your all's…. fuck 'em! You really had me thinking the timing was just wrong with us. You had me thinking we could've worked if we tried, but you aint want to be with Q! You are in some relationship *two* months after we ended! A fucking relationship!" she yelled at him.

"Are you gonna let me explain?"

"Explain, what? Ya lie?!"

"I didn't lie to you Mo. At the time, I didn't want to be in a relationship, but things changed."

She began doing her breathing techniques· "I don't care. I don't care. I don't care. I wish you the best in ya shitty life." She hung up the phone.

She thought if she deleted his messages, he'd leave her mind, but that aint how stuff works. Tangible things are not why Love entered the situation; it was feelings and feelings can't be deleted like pictures and messages and clothes. Her feet were planted.

But, I was tired of watching them. I mean, I appreciated being so close to Love, but I saw it as a waste of my time. Mo was pretending, and Q was being occupied.

I went back to my rock. Instead of sitting, I walked around.

"You aint quittin' on me, are you?" Love's voice approached from behind.

I turned around and saw her; "Can't lie to you Love, I'm about to be out."

She stood beside me, confused; "Quittin' is for cowards."

"And wasting time is for the foolish."

She rose her eyebrows at me; "What time you have?"

"Had a year, but since I've been hanging with you, I've missed two months."

"Call yourself having an attitude, huh?" she asked.

"It's not an attitude Love; I'm just tired of having false Hope. I believe in things that God has a different outlook on."

"You do know the closer you get to God, the more your heart shapes like His. No one told you to stop being His friend."

"Describe a friend to me."

"God."

I shook my head.

"Your word is all you have, and you're about to back out of it." She said to me.

Love looked at me like I meant something to her.

"I'm tired Love."

"Then go to sleep!"

"This aint a tired that sleep can cure. It's my soul."

"Then do some in house cleaning, but I'm not gonna let you quit."

She gave me three days. Told me that I could go anywhere in the world and she wouldn't bother me. So, I went to India Arie's spot; this place called Beautiful.

Not many are blessed enough to go; only the free can enter. I had to use Love's name to get in.

I was surrounded around peace, happiness, and understanding. I didn't feel like I was wrong for being lost. My mind wasn't moving uncontrollably. I could sit. Think. And I saw no sparkle; not because no one was in Love, but because in Beautiful everything you Hoped for comes true.

I'm talking about clean; every plant was unique. Every insect was amazing. And quality time; I was able to listen to me, to talk to me, explain to myself that I was mad, and I told myself, 'I had the right to be'.

While standing by the water, I looked over and saw Job. He spotted me and nodded his head. I waved. Didn't take long for him to slide over; "When'd you start coming here?"

"First time." I answered.

"Can you dig it?"

"Oh yeah", I looked around, "This is what I needed."

"How you get in?"

"Love."

He laughed; "Knew they wouldn't let you in by ya self."

"What's that supposed to mean?" I asked.

"You don't know how to fly."

He dug in his robe and pulled out a folded piece of paper with jagged edges. He handed it to me. I knew who it was from.

"No man." I handed it back.

"No one said you had to read it now. Got one more day here; read it when you get home." He began walking away.

"I don't plan on going back."

"You aint leaving Love."

And he was right. I enjoyed my last day.

When I got home, Love was sitting on my rock. I smiled when I saw her.

"I knew you'd be back." She stood up and came over to me. Her arms let me know that I was missed.

I inhaled her scent. Simplicity.

"How you feel?" she let me go.

I reached in my pocket and pulled out Mo's letter; "I don't know."

"Mo?" she asked.

I nodded my head.

"She wrote me one too."

"Was she mean?" I asked.

"Open it." Love began walking away.

I watched till she was out of my sight. Looked at the letter, wondering if Mo deserved to be given attention. But I remembered that she was one of my favorites, so I gave her respect.

November 9, 2016

You gotta understand that I'm young, and when I'm pissed, that no nice way of saying it. A heart break is every emotion at once, and my Mama aint warn me about this one. She taught me to avoid pain, but forgot to school me on how to deal with it when it comes.

I've never despised someone like I despise Q. Wouldn't call it hate cause that's a strong ass word, but I don't fool with him.

I was really trying to be a better person. I feel like Life said 'Oh, you think you're about to chill on cussin'? Q got a girl.' I mean, who wouldn't be pissed? You were there. You saw us. Tell me I was the only one to feel something and I promise, I'll...shave my head.

Love is unfair because I feel like she's only picking at me. I hear her. The little whispers she be doing, and it gets annoying.

Wonder how it'd be if she talked to me about me.

The truth is, my insides are tearing up. I never wanted something so bad that I can't have, and the worst part about it all, is Q doesn't want to be wanted by me. I thought I was valuable. I thought I meant something, but maybe I didn't. Maybe...every woman aint for every man. Learning this stuff hurts.

Imagining him with another girl makes my stomach turn. My issue with Q is if he didn't want anything from me, he shouldn't have approached me in the Library. I don't understand why people enter your life to fuck it up. I was fine without him.

You know how hard it is not be mad at God? Because besides you being there, I know for a fact God knew. It wasn't like I didn't talk to Him about Q; God knew that my feelings for him were true, and he didn't give a warning. Worst of all, He's been silent lately. At the time that I need my friend, He aint talking. And I know Him; I know deep, deep, deep down in my heart, God is still here, but sometimes it's hard to say that He is good.

I want to apologize to you for the last letter. You were the easiest person to blame, but I'm trying to take ownership of my part.

I thought that it was my attitude; I thought it was my fault why we ended. I mean, I was the one asking the questions and getting mad at his answers, but now, I see that he never wanted me. And the shit hurts.

But each day I try.

-Mo.

Her honesty cut me deep. I went to find Love. She was at a Lake.

"I wonder why it's encouraged for people to grieve about death, but not relationships ending." She started the conversation.

"People grieve about relationships ending." I held up Mo's letter.

"In privacy; as though tears are a sign of weakness."

"Who do you know, besides Boys ii Men, will get on their bended knee and put their pride aside?" I asked her.

"Keith Sweat. Jodeci. Tyrese. Barack Obama; there's no telling what that Man will do if Michelle left!"

I laughed; "Nah, when I hit them, I hit them hard. They're a forever thang."

She smiled.

"I read Mo's letter." I said.

"Did she cuss you out?"

"Nah", I shook my head, "She vented. Even apologized."

"My girl is growing."

"What she say to you?" I asked.

Love laughed; "Oh she said some words, then asked for my help."

"You gonna help her?"

"Oh yeah", Love nodded her head, "When someone allows me in, I tend to act up!"

I laughed; "I really appreciate you."

"You too Cupe."

So, we were back to business. Watching Mo and Q.

"You don't have others to tend to?" I asked Love.

"I move freely. Help when I can." She answered.

"Ever get tired of your job?"

"No." she shook her head.

"Discouraged?"

She smiled; "I attended this wedding. The woman said her vows to her husband and when it came time for him to say it to her, he stared in disbelief. The whole Church was confused, but the woman was used to the look. He shook his head and began crying; looked at the crowd and told them that 'she was his soul sister', so no, I don't get discouraged."

Love is my black butterfly.

They were comfortable with their lives. Mo felt the pain, but school distracted her. Q may have had a girl, but Mo's spot was still vacant.

Everything can't fit in the hole a person left. Love and I knew that, but Mo and Q didn't. I got frustrated; extremely tired of those two pretending, so I asked Love 'can I mettle'.

"You gotta ask God." She told me.

"…nah." I shook my head.

And I was glad I didn't ask Him, cause a couple days later, Q saw Mo on campus. She was walking to her car.

I don't know why he felt the need to call her name. Mo aint one to act nice when she's pissed. Wasn't a surprise that she rolled the hell out of her eyes.

"Damn." Q touched his chest.

Mo unlocked her door.

"Mo." Q ran up to her.

"This nigga has lost his mind." Mo opened her the door. She got in.

Q ran over. Stopped her from closing it; "Mo, damn."

"Q you four, five seconds to get away from my car 'fore I roll over yo' lyin' ass feet."

"*Damn*." Q let go of her door.

"Thank you so very much." She closed it. Q backed up.

She started her car, put it in reverse, and backed out the parking spot.

"Baby steps, baby steps." Love repeated.

I shook my head; "Mo is a piece of work."

"Q has to give her time to adjust. He wants everyone to be cool with him."

"Might want to chill on talking to Mo 'fore she beat him up."

"Might."

You'd think the car scene would make Q chill on talking about Mo, but nah. Lex ear was what he dug in.

"Why don't you just let Mo be?" she asked him while they sat at one of the Tables in the Cafe.

"You're saying it like I'm pressed. I aint pressed, I just want to know why she's mad." He drunk his Juice.

"Cause your dumb ass got a girlfriend after telling her you didn't want to be in a relationship!"

"Lex, I aint think Mo cared. Whole time we were talking, I was the one doing the work. Then she let the shit go like it was nothing. And hell, when I tried to talk to her, she either cussed me out or ignored my ass."

"You act like you 'ont know who this girl is! Did you really think it'd be easy for Mo to open up to you? And you know she's guarded as fuck; ya actions told her she had the right to be."

Q didn't respond.

"Have you apologized?" Lex asked.

"I aint lie to her."

"I don't think you did either; I believe you liked her, but…sometimes giving up is easier than making shit work."

"That's what you think. You know how annoyed I get when she ignores me?"

"Why do you care? Don't you have a girl?"

"Mo's cool people. I didn't want us to get together cause I aint know how we'd end. If I would've known shit was gonna be like this, I would've just---"

"Tried?" Lex asked.

He shrugged his shoulders; "A lot of stuff went unsaid."

"Then speak on 'em."

"You already know how Mo is."

"If you want to have that conversation with her, you're gone have to wait cause she is pissed at yo ass!"

"I hurt her?" he asked.

"What you think dumb ass."

"I swear I didn't mean to. None of it was done with malicious intents."

"Sometimes, it doesn't matter what you meant to do, but what you did."

He didn't say anything.

"Regret it?" she asked.

He looked at her; "You gonna go back and tell Mo 'bout this?"

"Nah", she shook her head, "Hearing your name pisses her off."

Love stayed with Q while I went to Mo. She was in the Library studying for her Chemistry Test. Her headphones were in her ears. Playing was David Ryan Harris song Don't Look Down.

She dropped her pencil and closed her book. Took a deep breath. She was sitting in a cubical, so her tears falling was still a secret.

Her heart weighed more than her entire body, causing her to drag. It's hard to act like Love isn't there when she keeps talking.

Mo took her headphones out of her ear and wiped her face.

November 16, 2016

I asked God to take the feelings away. He has yet to do so.

I have this Love that is pure. A Love where facades don't exist. I was exposed to it when I decided to walk away. Looked at it like 'Oh shit Mo, maybe you do have a heart'.

And when I was ready to give it to someone, it wasn't wanted.

I could give this boy things he didn't know existed, and he doesn't care to experience it. Worst part of it all, if he called right now and said, 'He wanted to give us a try', I'd be all in.

I don't think Love is stupid, I think we act stupid towards Love.
Lowkey tired of acting like a bad ass. Tired of holding tears in till it's time to go to sleep.

And sleep? What the hell is that? Q don't take over my mind until the lights go out.

I asked God to take the feelings away. They're still here.

-Mo.

I went to Love and told her about Mo's journal entry.

"Why didn't God take the emotions away?" I questioned.

"I asked Him not to." She answered.

"Why?"

"Cause she asked me to 'help her experience me with herself'."

I didn't say anything back because I knew what Love meant.

A heartbreak is something no one can heal. It takes Time. During that Time, the person must have their own back. Encourage themselves when they don't want to get out of bed, dress themselves when they feel like the ugliest thing on Earth, push themselves when they have no reason to move. Heartbreak isn't just about missing the person you "lost", but dealing with the emotions that comes along with that. Depression is easy to seep into. The sun gets on your nerves because it forces you to act happy. Rainy days are your best friend. And don't let it be a snow storm; gives you a reason not to leave the house.

Mo's eyes were tired, and I could tell.

Her soul. His soul. Life was moving, and secretly they missed each other.

Mo went to God about her pain.

"My issue isn't the heartbreak, but your silence through all of this. Why you aint talking to me? Why...am I at a place where I feel like all I have is Mo? My loyalty to you is deep; don't take me for granted."

Love sighed; "I need her to hold on."

"Give her a reason to."

"Say less."

Love went ghost for a couple days. Came back looking refreshed.

"Where you been?" I asked.

"Talked to God." She responded.

"'Bout what?"

"You'll see."

Mo decided that she wasn't gonna go to class. Needed a day off, so she laid in her bed and watched Movies.

BET played Sparkle. She sang along to the songs and smiled every time Derek Luke hit her screen.

When it got to the end, she stood up and put her remote to her lips. Her and Jordan Sparks were about to shut her Apartment down! Till, for the first time, she decided to listen to the words.

She stood there silently, as Jordan sung her heart out.

"Can't fly with one wing." Mo repeated.

She went to her desk and got out a sticky note. Wrote down the quote and then stuck it on her wall. She looked at it and then nodded her head; "A'ight God. I get it."

"Get what?" I asked Love.

She looked at me; "Remember that the sky aint a ceiling."

"What's up with the quotes?"

"Study 'em."

Mo stopped faking. The Truth was what she moved with. Cause reality was whether she wanted to feel for Q or not, she felt for him. So, she had to deal with it. Care for the Love scratch.

Meaning she had to look at it. Remember where it came from and why it was there. Was it so bad that she experienced Love? Because the truth is, not everyone gets to Love a good person.

Q made a wild decision, but his heart was the same as before.

Mo started noticing that her heartbreak was a blessing. It exposed her to things she didn't know she had. Like the ability to Love. The ability to want to communicate, to want something to work out. The heartbreak helped her relationship with God become an honest one; He was the only person she'd vent to.

"Lord, I'm not asking you to make things easy for me, but supply me with what I need to make it through the storm." She prayed.

"His grace is sufficient. You already got it." Love whispered to her.

Mo knew God deeper than Q, so that's why she couldn't pretend. I'm not saying he wasn't into his girl, cause he was, but he acted unbothered about Mo. Stopped saying her name when he bumped into her friends.

"How you and ya girl gone make it work when you leave?" Ryan asked him.

He shrugged his shoulders; "Just gone have to make the shit work."

"You happy, bruh?"

"Yeah; she's what I need right now. Keep me motivated."

"That's what's up."

I looked close to Q's chest and saw a speck of sparkle. Went to Mo and saw a piece in her hand.

"Love, I thought you never leave?" I asked her.

"I don't." she responded.

But I was confused, because everyone knows the smaller the sparkle, the less the feel. I wasn't ready to watch my arrows fail. Thought about going back to Beautiful.

"Cupid." I heard God call my name.

I ignored him.

"Cupid!" he repeated.

Still acted deaf.

He left me alone.

I wanted to take a day from those kids, so I told Love to 'let me take her to the Lake'.

She smiled; "Water?"

"You're with it?"

"Oh yeah."

She let me lead her. Watching Love admire the water reminded me of Halle Berry in 'Their eyes were watching God'.

She bent down to the water and put her hands in it; "What you takin' from me Cupe?"

"What you mean?" I watched her from a far.

She looked back at me; "Am I helping you?"

I shrugged my shoulders; "Giving me something to do."

"Have you thought on ya bow and arrow?" she asked.

"Nah." I walked over to her.

"Why not?"

I sat beside her; "A part of me feels like I had a role in this. I knew they weren't ready."

"Why don't you think they were ready?"

"Cause you can't pour from an empty cup."

Love sat beside me; "Mo and Q had everything to give. God knew they'd scare each other."

"Can you tell me if they're gonna work out?" I asked.

"I don't know", she shrugged her shoulders, "But Life is about growth; I'm about growth. And I know for sure these two are growing."

"Even Q?"

"Especially Q. I see his heart."

"It's possible that these kids are growing apart." I said.

"Or helping each other grow!" she smiled.

January 6th was the day for Q to head out to his internship. Chicago. Enough miles for him and Mo not to bump into each other.

"They think about one another?" I asked Love.

"What you think?"

I couldn't tell. Mo was serious about getting herself together, and Q was focused on his task. And their sparkles? Completely gone.

I hid my frustrations from Love, but when the sun fell, I called God's name.

It was quiet for a while, then Job showed up.

"My mans!" he approached me.

"You talked to God lately?" I asked.

"Oh yeah."

"He said anything about me?"

"Asked how you was doing. Told me to tell you 'He misses you'."

I took a deep breath; "Has He told you the purpose of all of this?"

"Mo and Q? Nah. Those kids story is…untold." He answered.

"Think I'm wasting my Time watchin' 'em?"

He shook his head; "Nothing is for nothing; even Moses had to lead the sheep before the Israelites. Just take it all in Cupe."

"It's, it's, its… a lot going on. Can I be honest with you?" I asked.

"Oh yeah."

"I thought Love never leaves, but those kids have no sparkle."

"Love sees below the surface. She doesn't leave."

"But I don't think they want each other anymore. Don't get me wrong, I'm sure they care for one another, but I think it's over."

"Nah, just that part."

"What part?"

"Be patient enough to see."

But patience is achieved by patient folks. I wanted to know what was up.

Peace was restin' with Mo. Her GPA was the focus.

"What you doing this weekend?" Ciara asked her.

"Got a paper."

"For the whole weekend Mo?!"

"Keep it real, I'm just chillin'."

"Damn girl. I'ma call Lex."

January 16, 2017

It's something about today that
makes me feel like I'll be alright. Life
aint changed; my perception of it has. I
remembered God when I was younger;
when a twenty-dollar bill was what we
had to eat off for a couple days. It's a
blessing to have a Mom who made it
through the struggle. She used to always
tell us 'make sure you prayin' cause God
is waiting'. Said that before saying
'Amen' you have to make sure you mean
what you're talking about'. But how do
you know, that you know, what you're
talking about, if you don't know? Cause
sometimes we ask God for things we
believe we want, until we get it. And
then there are times we really, really,
really want something and God will say
'No'. All He says is 'No', never explains.
Some say He shouldn't have to, because
your Faith in Him should be strong
enough for you to trust whatever He
says, but the Devil likes to yell at you.

Feeds off your Frustrations and make you think that you have the right to be pissed.

See my storm is deeper than Q and I. Cause these last couple months have changed me. First time having a room to myself ever, first time having a car ever, first time that I am in control of how I feel. I am in control of how I feel. And I'm learning how to take care of me; how to be there for me, give me whatever my soul needs to make it to the next day.

Times get hard, but the truth is, it is our light, not our darkness that scares us the most. And learning that helped me notice that I was far from ready with Q.

Love is an action that a selfish person cannot do. My name is Mo and I am selfish as hell. Selfish with my time and territorial with my Pride. But, I want to change.

So, last night, I wrote a note to Fear. Thanked him for allowing me to hide, but informed him that it was time for me to come out. And I know that Fear leaving makes me noticeable to my enemies, but I'll be damned if I treat my fence like aluminum foil; it aint gone move and I aint scared....so there's that.

-Mo.

"That's what I'm talking about!" Love smiled at Mo, noticing her Poker-face was leaving.

Honesty. Admitting that you are not okay. Responsibility. Fixing ya self.

Oh, how she was meditating. And reading. And resting. And talking. And moving. And eating. And crying. And drying them. And standing up. And having knee time, having Mo time.

Her four walls were amazed when she brought Beautiful into them.

Angels came to see what Job was talking about.

"Faith." An Angel stared at Mo.

"Yeah", Love smiled, "She is dope."

Dope enough to be easy on God's silence, but hard on her heart.

See, just because you admit to your heartache doesn't mean it goes away any faster.

She wondered about Q. Started calling herself crazy cause she still had feelings for someone who moved on.

But I saw no sparkle in Q. Not saying that he didn't Love his girl, but it's a fact that you can't sparkle when you Love two people at the same time. Don't know why; you just can't.

"Are they ever gonna talk again?" I asked Love.

"After I talk to them, they will." She answered.

But Love became silent. Said 'now was the time for Q and Mo to live in silence so their minds could be worked on'.

So, their minds could be worked on.

That replayed in my head over and over. I went back to my rock. Wondered if it was time for me to get my mind right.

I called God's name. Job showed up. I laughed, remembering that God comes in images we will listen to.

Entertained the conversation with Job. Then decided to go to God's office.

Walking there, I wondered what I would say. I didn't think I was wrong for wanting to put down my bow and arrows, nor did I want them back. But I wanted God to understand why I stopped talking to Him. I wanted Him to know that His place in my Life was needed, but we had to have an understanding. I needed Him to know who I was just as much as I wanted to know who He was.

"Who you think made you?" God asked, before I could say anything.

I didn't respond.

"I know you; knew that you were gone get frustrated, give me your arrows, and leave. I even know how this story ends. You're mad because you don't, but if you knew all that I know, you'd stop moving."

"Stop moving?" I asked.

"Pay attention to what's in front of you. And know that I am."

That was all we said to one another.

I didn't tell Love about God and I's conversation; really didn't know how to explain it.

God said: You'd stop moving. But I don't remember taking steps. For months, I was watching Mo and Q, so technically, I wasn't moving.

I got frustrated with God once again. His words came across as an insult to my intelligence.

But Mo. She explained it to me without even knowing.

"If I trust God, then I won't let my mind run me crazy." She told herself.

I made a mental note of it.

"Where's your sister?" I asked Love.

"Hope or Faith?" she responded.

I wondered which one would help the most; "Both."

"In your heart."

"Huh?"

She laughed; "Go to Freedom land. There, is a tunnel where everyone's hearts are. Go find yours, and call for Hope and Faith. They'll come."

"You got Mo and Q?" I asked.

"Of course."

7,200 minutes; also known as 5 days. That's how long it took me to reach Freedom land. Talked to a couple folks and they pointed me in the direction of the tunnel.

All the hearts were in the wall; names rested on each one.

I could tell by looking at them who had experienced what.

The blacker the heart, the darker the soul.

I reached mine. Noticed that the red was turning purple.

"Hope! Faith!" I yelled out.

Nothing happened.

"Hope! Faith!" I repeated.

Nothing happened.

I took a deep breath; "God, come on now."

"There you go!" a voice came from behind.

I turned around. Swore I was looking at Whitney Houston when she played Cinderella's Fairy God mother.

"Hope?" I asked.

She shook her head; "Faith."

"Where's Hope?"

"I'm coming!" Hope ran to us. She looked like Goapele.

"Dang, ya'll are some beautiful sisters." I said.

"Why thank you!" Faith smiled.

"Thought you were gonna force us out of your space." Hope added.

"That's why I'm here", I started, "I need ya'lls help."

"As if we didn't know!" Hope smiled.

"How close are ya'll to God?"

"His main squeezes!" Hope announced.

Faith laughed.

"Why?" I asked.

Hope shrugged her shoulders; "Why not?"

"…cause…sometimes…He…."

"Ain't clear?" Faith asked.

I nodded my head.

"Where many mess up at is putting Faith in things other than God." Hope said.

"Cause things fail; God doesn't." Faith added.

"And when Life seems to be going in a direction that doesn't seem good, having us in God will help you understand that today's sorrow is for tomorrow praise." Hope continued.

"So, you keep us close, but near the right things." Faith informed me.

"And move with Love." They said together.

"That easy?" I asked.

"That easy." Faith answered.

I left and went to find Love. She was watching Q order some jewelry online for his girlfriend's birthday.

"You talk to my sisters?" Love asked.

I looked at Love, noticing that her beauty matched theirs; "Who is ya'lls Mama?"

She laughed; "How was it?"

I smiled; "It was cool."

"That's good."

We watched Q. Though my eyes seemed to have been into his task, I was thinking about those dark hearts.

"So", Love began, "How many hearts would Ammut had enjoyed in that tunnel?"

"Mannn." I thought back to ancient Egyptian religion.

"Hearts looked heavier than a feather?" she asked.

"*My* heart looked heavier than a feather."

"Work on that, a'ight?" she asked.

"I got you."

But a Feather doesn't have weight, so how in the hell was I gonna do that?

I remembered that God said: Stop moving and pay attention to what's in front of you; so, I chilled. Watched the kids.

Mo's interaction with Peace were magical. Problems were around, but she had confidence. Bad news couldn't get to her.

Till Lex told her that 'Q came in town to surprise his girl'.

"Good for him."

"When was the last time Mo and Q saw each other?" I asked Love.

"Car scene."

I nodded my head. Wondered if they'd see each other and if so, how would it play out.

Of course, Lex had a function at her house that night. Told the whole crew. Q came. Mo didn't.

"I can't put myself in a situation where I'll probably fail." Mo told Ciara before she went out.

"Huh?" Cee asked.

"Q's in town."

"Girl, don't let that keep you in this house!"

There was nothing Ciara could say to make Mo leave the house. She didn't want to see Q, and she damn shou'll didn't want to see him with his girlfriend, so she smoked a blunt and then went to sleep.

Love went into her dream. Mo knew who she was.

"Yo, who told you, you could invade my space?" she asked Love.

"Pride moved aside, and I slid in." Love responded.

"Well slide the hell out."

"You already know I can't do that."

"You in Q's spot?" Mo asked.

"We aint talking about Q. I'm here regarding your rose."

"I don't even like flowers. What are you talking about?"

"I need you to grow."

"I have come a long way!" Mo rolled her neck.

"And you're going the wrong way. Don't sleep on Life."

Mo listened. She woke up.

2 o'clock in the Morning. They were separated, wondering what the other person was doing. Were they happy? Was Life going well? Did they cross each other's mind? If so, did they let them stay?

What is the use of a cellphone if you aint gone call?

Q left town.

Mo said "Goodbye" to her heartache.

The next day, it said 'Good morning'.

She was pissed.

"Yo Love, what we doing?" I asked.

"Hoping." She responded.

"For what?" I asked.

"The stems to pop out."

"Huh?" I asked.

"Spring is coming."

I was confused, so I left it alone.

Q coming in town messed Mo up. Had her mind moving real fast. Mary Jane couldn't slow it down.

Q's? He seeped into his distractions. The desire for success helped him focus on his internship. Every now and then, Mo would dig a hole in his heart. He stuffed his girlfriend in it. His heart rejected.

"You can't move on and think that the thing you didn't finish won't come up. Life don't work like that." Love said.

"Can you let them know?" I asked.

"They'll learn."

Mo's Mama called her.

"Hello?" Mo answered.

"Why you aint called me?!" her Mama asked.

"I don't know."

"Umm", her Mama poked out her lips, "That don't make no sense. What you doing?"

"Homework."

"…why you sound like that? What the hell wrong with you?"

"Nothing."

"Monica, don't play with me; what's wrong?"

"I don't want to talk about it Ma."

"Oh well, you have to! Tell me!"

"…God's been silent lately."

Her Mama understood; "But He hasn't left."

"Yeah, but every now and then, I need a word."

"Does the GPS talk when you're going in the right direction?"

"When I get to a turn, she does."

"A'ight then! Chill out, you got this!"

"…okay."

"Don't forget whose child you are. Everything you need to make it, He put in you. His Grace is sufficient; now you gotta believe it."

What a blessing it is to have Superwoman as your Mom.

So, Mo fought. Wasn't letting Pain get a hold of her soul. Love smiled at her. And when she needed a hug, Love gave it to her.

"You are the definition of a best friend." I told her.

"Why thank you!"

February 21, 2017

Thank Fantasia for telling me that it was necessary. Pain hurts bad when it's new. You walk and then began to fall, and people tell you to get up, but they can't tell you how to get up. So, if you must crawl until you can get to your feet, then it is okay to do so. I am supposed to endure my problems and learn how strong Grace is connected to me.

If God's grace is sufficient, then my problems are not as big as I thought they were. If God promised me Peace, then maybe that is what His silence is. Showing me, what Peace looks like.

My pain is a part of my process; learning how to deal with myself was the goal when God handed the trouble to me. He wants me to learn how to stand; how to deal with things that looks harder than me.

I must be confident in who I am. I must believe that God is the same friend

He was before. I must trust that He knows Love better than I.

The thing about rain is its only water. Why is it that I have learned to relax in the shower, but when Life rains on me, I become disconnected with who I am supposed to be?

I can no longer have the same mindset.

This is step one. Realizing that my way of thinking is killing my soul.

I ask Faith to stay close to me cause sometimes the Devil sounds real, real good. I allowed myself to listen to what he was saying, he asked 'where is my God'. I said, 'Right there'.

Friendship stays no matter the circumstances. There is nothing that can detach me from my friend. I prepared myself for this. I got this.

-Mo

Q was fighting too. He didn't believe in cheating; mental nor physical, but he was partaking in the activity. Mo sat on his mind like it was her bed.

He wanted to know how she was doing. Didn't want to ask Lex, wanted to know straight from Mo, but because she "hated him", he left it alone.

I caught him praying for her.

"Damn." I said, seeing what could've been.

Could've.

Should've.

Would've.

Mo didn't care what her mind imagined; reality was reality, and reality was, Q had moved on. So, she had to work through the pain.

She played with her feet a lot; back and forth, back and forth, back and forth.

"If she'd stop fighting, I could help her." Love said.

I can do things you haven't seen.

Introduce you to Hope while pushing Doubt out the door.

Your soul, I promise to care for.

But I need you.

I can introduce you to a new definition of best friend,

While taking "Just Fucking' out of your vocabulary.

Making Love.

Slowly.

Passionately.

Listen to me.

Whisper to me.

Vent...to me.

Allow me to introduce you to the things people write of,

Sing of,

Dream of,

I can introduce you to Life.

But I need you.

I can be the tissue to your tears,

The Faith to your Fears.

Let me be Love.

Let me add Jazz to your day,

A walk with a sway,

A smile that forbids frowns,

My friend, I need you.

I need you to look at those walls and question their
existence.

I need you to be quiet about your happiness because
Haters are real.

I need you to respect the night,

When all is silent, I need you to be thankful.

When arms are your Robitussin,

I need you to be thankful.

When "For better or for worst, till death do us part"

Is being said, I need you to be thankful.

I need,

You.

Don't curse me when you feel pain.

Patient.

Kind.

The truth.

That's what Cupid calls me.

I need you.

I need you to want for me as much as you hear about me.

I need you to value my name,

While canceling the game.

I need you to keep it real.

Allow the stu-stu-stu stuttering to come on in,

Cause that's what I can do.

I can be the root to your rose,

The glitter to your toes.

I can make you laugh.

Make you hope.

Make you believe.

But first, I need you.

So, don't call my name unless you're willing to pay the price.

How much?

Guess.

– Love.

What does it mean when Love says that she needs you? Let me finish the story.

"Call her." Love told Q.

"Nah." He responded.

I wanted to cuss him out. All Love had done for him and he told her 'no'. Not only was Love patient with him and Mo, but she was allowing him to experience something new without deserving it.

"Let me take you away from this place." I told her.

"If I leave, everything will end." She said.

"Then let it! You are Love, and you get the least appreciation."

"I'm not here to be praised, but to have my Garden all red."

"What garden?" I asked her.

"My rose garden."

"Where is it?"

"Oh, that's my secret." She smiled.

"So, I can't know?"

"Uh, ah." She shook her head.

"You ever been to Love's Garden?" I asked Job.

"No, I heard about it." he answered.

"Where is it?"

"I 'ont know, but I heard that there's no dirt there."

"What is a Garden without dirt?"

"Only has concrete."

"Roses growing out of concrete?" I asked.

"Only person Love let go with her was Tupac."

"So, Love has a Garden with roses growing out of concrete?"

"And every rose represents the people she whispers to. The more they listen to her, the more the seed grow."

"That is some dope stuff." I was amazed.

"We're talking about Love here. She's as dope as they come."

"Call Lex." Love told Q.

He did that.

"Baby steps." She said.

"Yo, Yo, yoooo!" Lex answered the phone.

"What you been up to?" he asked.

"Chillin' Man. Straight chillin'."

He laughed; "Do somethin' with ya life Lex."

"Man, what you want?!"

"Just callin' to see how everyone's doing."

"Well Mo is fine!" she knew why he called.

"I aint say Mo's name."

"I've known you since we were little; I know you!"

"…she's good though?" Q asked.

"I'm guessin'. She's been ghost lately."

"You haven't checked on her?"

"I go over and chill with her and Cee. Mo's chillin'.'"

"What does that mean?"

"She's chillin' nigga! She's good!"

"Oh, a'ight."

"…why 'ont you call her?"

"For her to cuss me out? Nah."

"She might surprise you."

"I know Mo. She probably won't answer the phone."

"Maybe", Lex said, "But what's up with you and ya girl? Ya'll good?"

"Yeah."

"Then why you askin' about Mo?"

"She was my dawg Man; been on my mind lately."

"Time will come where ya'll will be cool." She said.

"Maybe."

Lex told Mo about the conversation her and Q had. Not trying to be messy, but let her know that he still cared.

"Who?" Mo acted like she didn't know who Q was.

"Don't be like that Mo."

She rolled her eyes.

Two steps back.

Three steps forward.

Q's name.

One step back.

A week Q free.

One step forward.

A picture of him.

Five steps back.

Shopping trip.

Three forward.

Their song.

Four back.

A crush.

Two forward.

A crush with stinky breath.

One back.

A new sex toy.

Two forward.

A new crush.

One forward.

A new crush with a cute smile.

One forward.

A crush who's crushin' back.

Three forward.

A crush with good sex.

Five forward!

Q coming back in town.

Square one.

"Shit!" Mo.

But that visit, Lex made sure they saw each other. She wasn't trying to be messy, but a good friend.

Told Mo 'she needed her to braid her hair in cornrows' and Q, 'she needed him to look at her washing machine'.

Q pulled up first. Then Mo.

He saw her park her car. Thought about going over, but remembered how her mouth works.

"I aint in the mood to get cussed out." He said to himself.

"So?" Love shrugged her shoulders.

He got out of his car and went to hers.

"Relax." Love told Mo.

She didn't know what Love was talking about, until she put her head up and saw Q standing at her door.

"What the hell?" she looked at him.

He motioned for her to roll down her window.

"Uh, ah." She shook her head.

"Be nice." Love told her.

Mo smacked her teeth while rolling down her window; "What's up?"

"How you been?" he asked.

"Good." She looked at him.

He waited for her to ask it back, but noticed who he was talking to; "Well I'm good."

"...I don't remember asking."

"Monica!" Love shook her head.

She took a deep breath, remembering that she was supposed to be a better person; "I'm glad you've been good."

Q laughed; "You know how hard it is for me to believe that?"

"I do not care."

He relaxed his back on Mo's car; "What you been up to?"

She reached her hand out the window and pushed him off her car; "Step back!" She turned her car off, unbuckled her seat belt, and then got out. Q noticed that her ass had grown.

"Lex told you to come?" he asked, while closing her door.

"Yeah."

She remembered that Q was a sweet guy, so chilled with her attitude.

They started walking to Lex Apartment.

"How's school?" He asked.

"I'm still beefin' with Professors, but my grades are good."

Q laughed.

"Your internship?" she questioned.

"A lot of work, but I got it."

Mo nodded her head; "That's what's up."

Q wished they could do that more often. He missed talking to her.

That interaction went well. So good that both their hearts went down memory lane.

"Get ya self together." -Q.

"No; remember reality." -Mo.

They both squared up with Love. She gave them what they asked for. An ass whoopin'.

March 16, 2017

I met a new guy. His name is Phil. He is amazing; I gave him the name of being my friend.

...thought I was moving on from Q, and then I saw him.

I am tired of picking myself up, just to fall when Q is near. I need the day to come where seeing him doesn't make my stomach drop. Where he'll just be a "once upon a time" and not my fairy tale ending. I'm trying to be patient, but time aint really movin'.

So, what in the hell am I supposed to do?

-Mo.

They both healed from their ass whooping and made a deal with Love.

"If you don't say anything about Mo/Q, we can be cool."

"Deal...for now." Love responded.

They left each other's minds which gave them time to be happy in their new situations.

"Teach me how to meditate." Phil said while Mo laid on her rooms floor. He sat on her bed.

"No." she looked at him.

"Why?!" he got up and laid beside her.

"Cause you're silly. You'll mess up the concentration!"

He laughed; "I can be serious sometimes Mo."

"When?" she rolled her neck.

He kissed her lips; "Come on baby, teach me how to meditate!"

She sat up, "Okay, but take me serious!"

"Gotchu, gotchu."

Mo let go with Phil. Guess she learned some lessons from Q.

"When something feels good, you just go with it." Mo vented to Ciara.

"So, you like him a lot?" Cee asked.

"I do."

"Gone punk out this time?"

"...nah."

"Why couldn't she do that with Q?" I asked Love.

"It wasn't a part of their story." She answered.

April 15, 2017

I wished that I would've appreciated what Q and I had when it was here, but that's the past. I now promise myself that I will not allow a good time to scare me. I'm not messing this thing up with Phil. I'm relaxing. Taking in that I have a connection with someone I enjoy; someone who is not only my boo, but my friend.

So, hell, why not? Already felt a heart break, making it through, and learned that what doesn't kill you makes you stronger.

But best believe I told Phil that if he thinks he can break my heart and move on, I'm committing murder. He laughed. Hope he knows I'm dead serious.

-Mo.

Lex birthday was coming up. Already know she was ready to get turn't. Told everybody to mark their calendars, and of course they did!

21 doesn't come around every Blu moon. While Lex thought she was gonna turn up at the club, her friends put their money together and bought a building for the night.

Course Q came back in town!

But him and Mo weren't thinking about each other. Figured that their feelings had left, but they confused Love's silence with abandonment.

Mo and Ciara kept Lex occupied while their other friends decorated the building.

Everyone on Campus knew about the party but Lex.

For once, no one was spilling water.

"I'm try'na figure out why ya'll two are the only ones I've heard from all day!" Lex shouted while sitting at their house.

"You don't like hanging with us?" Mo asked.

"Ya'll cool, but damn, it's my birthday!"

Ciara thought it was funny that Lex had no idea.

Phil knocked at the door. Mo knew it was him, so she got up to answer it.

Phil is the main one who can't hold water, so Mo knew to take him to her bedroom and close the door.

, "She still doesn't know?" he asked, pertaining to Lex.

"No, and make sure you don't say anything!"

"Baby, I got you." He laughed.

"What you gonna wear?"

"What you gono woar?! No ass shakin', a'ight?" he said.

"Not even on you?"

"Only on me!" he pulled her close.

They forgot about Lex and Ciara.

Birthdays represent how much ya friends Love you. Lex got a special place in a lot of folk's heart, so she had a good time!

The party was jumpin'. Even Love and I was jammin'.

I noticed Mo and Phil battling each other when songs like 'Soulja Boy' came on. I couldn't help but laugh.

Q's girl aint big on parties, so he left her at a table while he caught up on some fun. Ended up seeing Mo. Took him a minute to notice Phil.

He grabbed Ryan and asked, 'who that'.

"Mo's boyfriend." Ryan answered.

"Boyfriend?"

"Well…probably aint her boyfriend, boyfriend but they be together all the time."

Q got a good look at Phil.

"Corny." He said.

Ryan laughed; "Man, just have a good time tonight!" Went to get his boy a shot.

"I gotta go to the bathroom." Mo told Phil.

"Gonna get one of ya girls?" he asked.

Mo looked for Ciara. Spotted her by Ryan, which meant she was by Q; "Yeah, I'll be right back."

She walked over to them; "Hey ya'll", she smiled.

Q still had an attitude about Phil, so smiling wasn't what he was gonna do.

"What's up?" Ryan nodded his head.

Mo touched Ciara's arm; "Can you come to the bathroom with me?"

"Yeah."

They moved through the crowd.

By the time they got back to Q and Ryan, Q's girl was beside him. Mo could tell who she was by the way she clung to Q.

"That's cute." She said while passing.

Q heard her. He watched as she walked to Phil.

Jealousy entered the party. Went back and forth with Q and Mo.

"Talk to each other." Love told them.

"Nah." They both responded.

"So much for your roses growing out of concrete." I said.

"Don't underestimate me."

Black Butterfly

Fall 2018